SEWING: GRANDMA'S SPECIAL TRICKS

QUICK GUIDE TO LEARN TO DEVELOP YOUR FASHION DESIGN FOR READY-TO-WEAR RESULTS! START MASTERING YOUR SEWING MACHINE LIKE YOUR GRAMMY DO!

ELEANOR NELSON

CONTENTS

Introduction v

1. Accurate Measurements: 1
2. The Special Techniques of Sewing 13
3. Maintenance 39
4. Step-By-Step Sewing Projects (27 Projects) 44

Conclusions 91

© **Copyright 2021 by Eleanor Nelson- All rights reserved.**

This document is geared towards providing exact and reliable information in regard to the topic and issue covered.

- From a Declaration of Principles which was accepted and approved equally by a Committee of the American Bar Association and a Committee of Publishers and Associations.

In no way is it legal to reproduce, duplicate, or transmit any part of this document in either electronic means or in printed format. All rights reserved.

The information provided herein is stated to be truthful and consistent, in that any liability, in terms of inattention or otherwise, by any usage or abuse of any policies, processes, or directions contained within is the solitary and utter responsibility of the recipient reader. Under no circumstances will any legal responsibility or blame be held against the publisher for any reparation, damages, or monetary loss due to the information herein, either directly or indirectly.

Respective authors own all copyrights not held by the publisher.

The information herein is offered for informational purposes solely and is universal as so. The presentation of the information is without contract or any type of guaranteed assurance.

The trademarks that are used are without any consent, and the publication of the trademark is without permission or backing by the trademark owner. All trademarks and brands within this book are for clarifying purposes only and are owned by the owners themselves, not affiliated with this document.

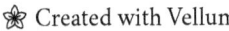 Created with Vellum

INTRODUCTION

Sewing is quickly becoming one of the worlds' most popular crafts again. The rise in the cost of living and the average drop or stagnation of wages means we can't always afford to go out and buy what we want. Whipping up a dress, skirt, or even a t-shirt that looks like it came out of an expensive boutique is not difficult if you concentrate and put your mind to it. As you have seen, it is better to learn how to sew using both a machine and by hand as you can use a combination of the two skills when making your creations.

All the topics covered in the book are truly meant for helping our readers in establishing a firm practice about the art of sewing. So you need to give a look at all these chapters so that any critical chapter cannot be overlooked.

But the direct explanation increases the speed throughout the following chapters. The basis of starting with the introductory information is very logical. It is projected to set up all the readers completely familiar with the thought of the topic.

The book starts with a brief but elaborative note about

INTRODUCTION

the basic concepts of sewing. So all you need is to first grab all these concepts and then move on to learning the practical features. The concepts are mentioned in a way that will be beneficial to apply in the practical aspect of sewing. The discussion then extends to the sewing tools and devices, so that the reader can easily apply the concepts in judging the right type of tool.

ACCURATE MEASUREMENTS:

How to Do It!

TAKE Accurate Measurements

Taking accurate measurements is also essential when it comes to sewing so that you don't waste time, effort, and of course, needles, thread and fabric. This chapter will provide you with a quick guide about the proper measurements of garments and pillow covers, as well as how to correctly take body measurements for sewing clothing. Check the guidelines out below.

Pillow Cover Measurements

Pillow covers are some of the easiest and most affordable sewing projects you can undertake. Here's a list of various types of pillows and their corresponding measurements.

Standard Pillow

- Dimensions: 20x26 inches
- Amount of Fabric Needed: 5/8 yard

Square Pillows

There are different dimensions for these, as you can see below:

- 30x30 inches—1 yard
- 20x20 inches—¾ yard
- 18x18 inches—5/8 yard
- 16x16 inches—½ yard
- 14x14 inches—½ yard
- 12x12 inches—1/3 yard

Queen Size Pillows

- Dimensions: 20x30 inches
- Amount of Fabric Needed: 1 and 1/8 yards

King Size Pillows

- Dimensions: 20x36 inches
- Amount of Fabric Needed: 1 and 1/8 yards

GARMENT MEASUREMENTS

Taking measurements for garments can be tricky because of the wide variety of both sizes and types of clothing. But it's good to have a guide to give you an idea of estimated measurements that could work for different body types, like the one below.

Long-Sleeved Dress with Skirt

- 35 to 36 inches—5 yards
- 44 to 45 inches—3 and 5/8 yards
- 50 inches—3 and ¼ yards
- 52 to 54 inches—3 and 1/8 yards
- 56 to 60 inches—3 yards

Short-sleeved dress with Straight skirt

- 35 to 36 inches—4 and ¼ yards
- 44 to 45 inches—3 and 1/8 yards
- 50 inches—2 and ¾ yards
- 52 to 54 inches—2 and 5/8 yards
- 56 to 60 inches—2 and 3/8 yards

Bias Cut Camisole

- 35 to 36 inches—1 and 1/3 yards
- 44 to 45 inches—1 and 1/3 yards
- 50 inches—1 and ¼ yards
- 52 to 54 inches—1 and 1/8 yards
- 56 to 60 inches—1 yard

Cap-Sleeved Blouse

- 35 to 36 inches—1 and 1/3 yards
- 44 to 45 inches—1 and 1/3 yards
- 50 inches—1 and ¼ yards
- 52 to 54 inches—1 and 1/8 yards
- 56 to 60 inches—1 yard

Long-Sleeved Blouse with Tie

- 35 to 36 inches—3 and 3/4 yards
- 44 to 45 inches—2 and 7/8 yards
- 50 inches—2 and 5/8 yards
- 52 to 54 inches—2 and 3/8 yards
- 56 to 60 inches—2 and 1/4 yards

Long-Sleeved Shirt/Blouse

- 35 to 36 inches—2 and ½ yards
- 44 to 45 inches—2 and 1/8 yards
- 50 inches—1 and 3/4 yards
- 52 to 54 inches—1 and 3/4 yards
- 56 to 60 inches—1 and 5/8 yards

Short-Sleeved Shirt/Blouse

- 35 to 36 inches—2 yards
- 44 to 45 inches—1 and 5/8 yards
- 50 inches—1 and ½ yards
- 52 to 54 inches—1 and 3/8 yards
- 56 to 60 inches—1 and ¼ yards

Softly Gathered Skirt

- 35 to 36 inches—2 and ¼ yards
- 44 to 45 inches—1 and 3/4 yards
- 50 inches—1 and 5/8 yards
- 52 to 54 inches—1 and 1/2 yards
- 56 to 60 inches—1 and 3/8 yards

A-Line Skirt

- 35 to 36 inches—2 and ¼ yards
- 44 to 45 inches—1 and 3/4 yards
- 50 inches—1 and 5/8 yards
- 52 to 54 inches—1 and 1/2 yards
- 56 to 60 inches—1 and 3/8 yards

Straight Skirt

- 35 to 36 inches—2 yards
- 44 to 45 inches—1 and 5/8 yards
- 50 inches—1 and 1/2 yards
- 52 to 54 inches—1 and 3/8 yards
- 56 to 60 inches—1 and 1/4 yards

Bermuda Shorts

- 35 to 36 inches—2 and ½ yards
- 44 to 45 inches—2 and 1/8 yards
- 50 inches—1 and 7/8 yards
- 52 to 54 inches—1 and 3/4 yards
- 56 to 60 inches—1 and 1/4 yards

Capri Pants

- 35 to 36 inches—2 and 3/4 yards
- 44 to 45 inches—2 and ¼ yards
- 50 inches—2 and 1/8 yards
- 52 to 54 inches—2 yards
- 56 to 60 inches—1 and 1/2 yards

Full-Length Pants

- 35 to 36 inches—3 and 1/4 yards
- 44 to 45 inches—2 and 5/8 yards
- 50 inches—2 and 5/8 yards
- 52 to 54 inches—2 and 1/4 yards
- 56 to 60 inches—2 and ¼ yards

HOW TO TAKE ACCURATE BODY MEASUREMENTS

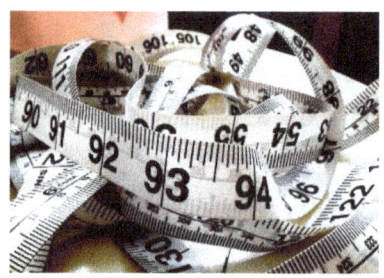

Basically, you need to take the following six measurements:

- Height: Stand barefoot with your back to a flat wall. Measure from the floor to the top of the head.
- Bust: Measure at the fullest part of the chest, making sure to keep the tape snug and even as you

wrap it around the back. Your arms should be at your sides while you are being measured.
- Waist: Measure at the natural waist (the narrowest part of the torso). Tie a string or ribbon at the natural waist and keep it in place for measurement #5.
- High bust: Lay the tape just above the bust and wrap it under the arms and straight across the back.
- Back waist length: Measure from the base of the neck to the natural waist (marked with the ribbon or string).
- Hip: Wrap the tape measure around the widest part of the hips or at least 7 inches below the waistline.

Notes:

Make sure that the torso and the floor are parallel to each other as you measure the subject.

Measure the subject while he is only in his underwear or while wearing a leotard for more accurate measurements.

And don't try to take your own measurements. This will only yield inaccurate results.

Common Mistakes

Being a beginner in anything is not always easy, and mistakes are made from time to time. If you have already made some mistakes, there is no need to worry because this is how you will learn and have an easier time in the future. Here is a list of some of the common mistakes that tailors make at the beginning. Knowledge of these errors will help you avoid them for a quieter beginning:

Purchase patterns that need to be modified

Sewing beginners are always looking for things to try, and sometimes you might be lured into buying patterns that will require significant alterations. This isn't a big problem for experienced tailors because they can alter any design perfectly, but this can be frustrating, time-consuming, and discouraging for a beginner. The final thing you need is to spend so much time on a project that won't go the way it should just because you can't make the proper alterations. Beginners learn best when they start simple projects; then, they can progress slowly instead of taking on big projects while still learning the basics.

Starting with a costly sewing machine

There is a common belief that more expensive sewing machines are the best to use because they have more features and are much easier to handle than other machines. This is not true, especially for beginners. A beginner should start on a simple sewing machine that can meet their learning needs and begin their first projects, and then maybe you can get a better sewing machine once you have mastered some complex techniques that require the use of more advanced machines. Also, an expensive sewing machine does not mean that it is the best on the market. You should always have in mind the quality of the machine and your current needs. It is elementary to get a good sewing machine to start sewing without spending so much money on it.

IGNORE FABRIC SUGGESTIONS **on patterns**

Every pattern will come with fabric suggestions. There are specific types of fabrics that are good for certain patterns. You need to understand this so you don't make a mistake that can ultimately ruin your project. Working with suitable fabric always contributes to the success of your sewing projects.

WORKING **on more than one project at the same time**

This is a widespread mistake with many tailors, not just beginners. Experienced tailors can probably handle more than one project on the go, but a beginner might not be. Beginners are moved by the excitement of starting to sew and learning many things at the same time, and this is what can quickly push you to take on more than one project at a time. The best thing for any newbie is to start one project, finish it, and then move on to the next.

The reason for this is that there is always something new to learn from your first project. You'll learn some skills and techniques and learn from some mistakes, which can help you improve things in your second project. Again, once you finish your first project, you can be sure that you will always finish other projects in the future.

BUY **a lot of things before you start**

This is also a result of the excitement to get started. Many people buy a lot of fabric, patterns, and even notions before even beginning their first project. These will overwhelm you so much and push you so hard to sew things that you haven't even learned how to sew. You need to take your sewing one step at a time. Even if things are on sale, you need to know that they will be on sale again in the future, probably at a time when you need them. Relax and only purchase what you need at that time. Once you learn a new skill, buy the fabric you need and work on it. This will also save space and ensure that you are an organized tailor from the order onward.

Downloading complex patterns without guidance

Nowadays, there are many sewing patterns you can download from the Internet in PDF format, and they can help you make great designs. The problem comes when you download too many patterns without a guide. That means you'll have to figure things out on your own, which is time-consuming and frustrating. You'll find great patterns that you can't even design because you don't know-how. This is not good for a beginner; you need to download patterns that come with instructions to save time and for quick learning.

Using the wrong tools

Many people don't take the time to gather all the tools they need to start sewing and start looking for other tools instead of the actual ones. This is a mistake that can mess up your first few projects, and this can kill your motivation to sew. The problem is that fundamental sewing tools are meant to make things easier for you and help you work faster. In your effort to save money on the right sewing tools, you end up compromising on time and effort. In the end, you won't enjoy sewing as much since you're taking more time on projects than you should, and maybe you keep making endless mistakes. To avoid all this frustration, invest some money in good sewing tools.

IT DOESN'T TAKE **time to learn a sewing machine**

This is a primary tool you will always use; therefore, it should be the first thing you master, even before learning your first sewing skill. You need to take the time to learn how to thread, for example. Practice a few times always to thread when required without wasting so much time on it. Learn everything about your machine beforehand, including all the features and how they work.

THE SPECIAL TECHNIQUES OF SEWING

The Special Techniques of Sewing
In the last section, we have made an effort for all the beginners so they can easily understand the basics of seaming and stitching. But for a learner, this is not enough. One needs to move forward for enhancing the special techniques of sewing and stitching.

Hemming

Hemming is needed at the end of the trousers, necklines and at the end of sleeves. Moreover, the raveling of fabric can be avoided by making beautiful hemming. Following are the major steps of hemming:

Turn around your fabric to an appropriate seam allowance. In most cases, a turn of ¼ inch will be enough. Now, when you have turned the edge equally, you need to press the fabric over the turn. It will give the fabric, a settled and pressed look.

Pinup the folded portion in a way that the fabric gets settled in your hand. Moreover, if you add too many pins, it will eventually disturb you in sewing, so you need to make an accurate adjustment in this regard. Now stitch at the pressed folds.

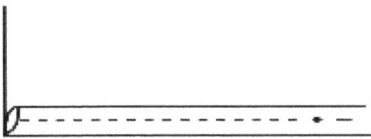

THERE MAY BE cases when you will need softer hems. In all these instances, you will make your hem through the hand using a needle and the thread.

Use Two Threads for Creating a Gathering

The gathering technique in sewing is basically used for all those accessories and dresses which need a little ruffle. It creates marvelous fullness in skirts, sleeves and hats. But applying the gathering technique needs some extra fabric, so it is necessary that, if your plan is to go for the gathering, you must plan it ahead, so that you are equipped with all the necessary items and fabrics, well before time. Gathering can be either light or intense, and in both cases, the quantity of fabric needed will vary.

SEWING: GRANDMA'S SPECIAL TRICKS

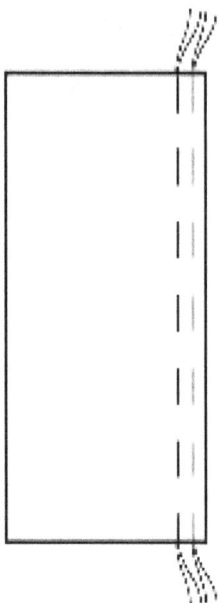

IN THE GATHERING TECHNIQUE, the first step is to have a correct seam allowance. One thing which people usually forget is a double seam allowance. As there will be a double seam for gathering, you need to keep your seam allowance double than normal.

Another technique used in the gathering is the one known as basting. For that, you need to keep your stitch length as long as possible.

Now, make the first seam along the length of the cloth at a width of ¼ inches. Now, when you are completed with the first seam, make another seam at a distance of ¼ inches. Now you will get two consecutive seams. But be careful to not cut off the threads at the end of each seam. These threads will be used to create the gathers.

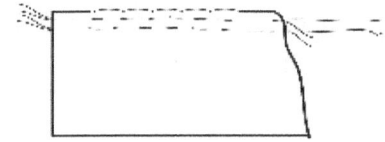

Now, when done with seams, gently pull off the threads from one end, by keeping a hand on the other. Gentle pulling will enable the gathering to be created. Now adjust the gathering in such a way that the gathers are adjusted evenly on the fabric.

Another technique is to pull the threads from both ends so that you can get more saturated gathers.

Appliqué Work

This is a very beautiful pattern-making technique, which can be added to the decorative ability of your dress or any other accessory.

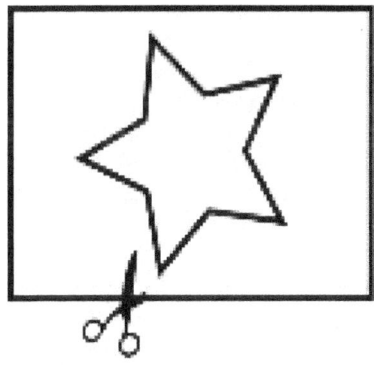

CUT the shape of the cloth into different designs. These will be the designs appearing as the pattern on another cloth. So cut the shape very finely.

NOW YOU WILL PUT the cut piece on the fabric, on which you want to paste the desired shape. The market is full of different products which can help you to enhance the ability of the cut piece to get stuck to the fabric. One such product is called "fusible web."

Use a zigzag stitch in order to keep it firm, cut the pattern in place. Stitch around the corners, alongside the edges, so that the shape cannot get distorted. One trick here is to keep the zigzag stitch only on the piece placed on the fabric. Do not stitch your underneath fabric along.

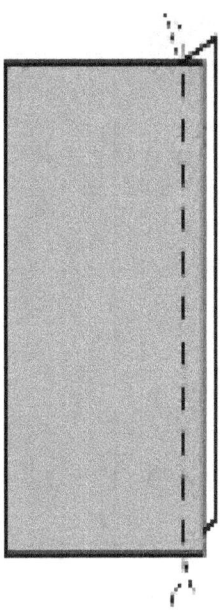

FRENCH SEAM

French seams are also another beautiful style for making your dress extremely decorative and stylish. The French seam will prevent any kind of ravel of the fabric so you can easily prevent it by just a simple trick of this kind of seaming.

SEWING: GRANDMA'S SPECIAL TRICKS

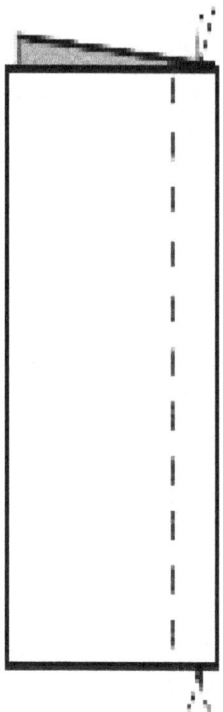

FIRST OF ALL, turn your fabric to the wrong side and stitch it to the end.

Now, turn it to the right side and make another stitch till the end of the fabric. Make sure that the second seam is apart from the first seam and it makes use of the distance left between.

These were a few of the sewing techniques which are largely used in a number of different sewing techniques. Although these have been provided with a step-by-step approach, yet you can also make your own innovative styles by the hit and trial method.

Flat-Felled Seams

These seams are common in men's wear. Their main purpose is to add a clean and professional look to the final item whenever you are sewing up shirts, sportswear and other garments. This is a strong seam, hence durable, and it will give your garment more structure without requiring you to add more bulk to the garment.

This is how it is done—one edge is folded over the edge of the other raw end, then it is topstitched down flat.

This kind of seam will work perfectly on reversible garments that are meant to look the same on both sides. If you are sewing a garment with tight curves, you should not use these seams.

Bias Bound Seams

Bias seams are also called the Hong Kong seam finish. They are basically an easy way you can add up a level of expertise to a garment that you are sewing. This is a great way to add some color to the insides of your projects in order to make them more appealing.

A raw edge of the fabric is encased completely in a strip of bias tape, which leaves a clean look on the inside of your garment.

This seam will not be easy but learning it will be great since you can always add something beautiful to your projects to make them more appealing. This technique is best done on heavy garments or those garments that do not have a lining.

Using a Rotary Cutter

Every tailor will need a rotary cutter and a cutting mat. However, you have to learn the skill of cutting with a rotary cutter to be able to use these invaluable tools effectively. A rotary cutter will always help you cut out patterns more easily, at a faster speed and perfectly. The cutting mat will help you protect your work surface from unnecessary cuts.

The rotary cutter should always be kept sharp, therefore you might have to keep a stock of rotary blades so that you can always change them to suit your sharp preference.

Princess Seams

These are basically a variation of darts that are used to create rounded curves that give shape to women's clothing. What you achieve through princess seams is an elongated, slimming appearance that should be tailored to the wearer in mind. These kinds of seams are perfectly used in fitted dresses and jackets in order to bring out a snugly contoured bust and waist. They are common in bridal gowns and couture dresses although they are slowly gaining popularity in most women's dresses.

There are a variety of other decorative seams that are available in most modern sewing machines that you can use in order to bring the best out of every project that you work on.

PRESSING and Ironing

Ironing is an important part of sewing as it helps to remove any wrinkles on a garment that you are working on. Ironing is very different from pressing, although both of them use an iron box, pressing is the recommended technique in sewing. Ironing, which involves gliding the iron back and forth the garment, can be damaging to the garment, which is why pressing is more recommended for sewing garments. Pressing involves placing the iron on the fabric and leaving it there for just a few seconds, then removing it. Pressing will not distort the fibers of your garment or fabric and it will help to set and blend your stitches for you to get a nice, crispy seam thereafter. You have to take proper care of your fabric or garment when pressing all the time.

Clipping Corners and Curves

This is a very simple but important technique that can help a lot when you are sewing. Seaming projects that have corners and curves is not an easy thing, and on such projects, you have to fight hard to keep the garment in place at all times. Clipping corners and curves can help ease up the work for you.

Clipping a corner at a diagonal, just close to the seam but not too close, will get you a nice and easy corner to work on and it will be perfect when you turn your project right side out.

Do the same for curves as well. Those curves that look like mountains can be notched and those that look like valleys can be clipped for ease of work and a perfect finish.

Stay Stitching

This is the technique that will help you prevent any kind of distortion on your curves. Stay stitching is done on a curve and it entails setting your stitch length to say 1.5, then starting your stitching on 1/8 inch from your stitching line.

Curves should be stitched immediately after they are cut in order to avoid distortion because moving your fabric a few times after cutting is enough to mess up your curve.

Fussy Cutting

This is a technique that you will use on a patterned fabric that you want to work on in order to isolate a motif. This is a much easier way to create easy appliques that will be added to the garments or projects that are meant for home décor.

In order to get the best cut, cut roughly around the motif that you want to isolate, ensuring that enough room is left out. Now trim the motif to its actual size leaving out a small seam allowance. Now you can place the motif on the fabric and to keep it in place, you can use satin stitches around it or use a spray adhesive.

Use of Bar Tracks

Bar tacks are used to reinforce the areas that could receive a lot of stress once the project is done. These areas are, for instance, pocket openings. Without the reinforcement, these areas will get weaker by the day and this can damage the garment. Bar tracks can be done using your sewing machine using a zigzag stitch or you can sew up by hand using a whip stitch.

Fabric Layout

Before laying out your fabric, make sure that you have got plenty of space to work, like a large table with appropriate height. Height does matter a lot as long as it is a good height that is suitable for your back.

A sewing table can be roped in as its height is higher than a normal table. Since the job of sewing requires a lot of attention to the minutest levels, doing it on a floor will lead to a sore back and painful leg muscles.

Every important element must be assembled beforehand like pattern pieces, lay-out directions, pins, scissors and fabric. Some important issues related to the laying of the fabric are as follows:

Stretching It Back into Shape

Take your fabric and fold it in the same fashion as shown in your pattern directions before laying it on a cutting surface. At times, if you don't get your fabric nicely laid in a line on the surface, it may be a bit stretched out of shape. If such is the case, try stretching the fabric slightly along the diagonal.

With the help of some other person, make the stretching from one corner to the opposite corner in the same direction in which requires adjustment. Another option to counter this problem is pre-washing, which is an effective solution.

The grain usually runs along the length of the fabric in parallel to selvages with the greater stretch running in the opposite direction i.e. perpendicular to the selvages. Note that they are the side edges of the fabric. Note the distance between them is the width of the fabric 45", 54", or 60".

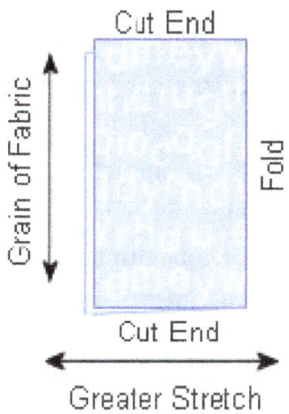

STRETCH OF FABRIC VS. GRAIN

Following the layout according to the correct direction is extremely important. Different fabrics have different directions for stretching. For example, you may want to stretch across the back of a skirt.

On the other hand, there may be some areas in which you would like to lessen the stretch, such as the length of the skirt. The pattern pieces will be finely and clearly marked regarding the direction they should be laid in. Have a look at the diagram given alongside.

The direction of the greatest stretch shown here may not be compulsorily correct. It may just be the opposite of this. To confirm this, hold your piece of fabric in two places, 1" apart. Pull the points apart from each other and measure the length of the stretch. Repeat the same procedure for the opposite direction and compare the two stretches. Take note of the greatest stretch and place the pattern pieces accordingly.

Fabric Cutting

Before you start with the cutting process, it is necessary to position all the pieces in the correct order. This also ensures that you have a complete understanding of the layout and there is enough space available for all the pieces to work upon. If you are a beginner, you better stick to the layout directions as given, following them in letter and spirit.

Once you start gaining experience, you may have your own way of laying out the pieces. After this is done, you must secure your pattern in the right place before starting off with the cutting procedure. For this, you'll be needing pins and weights. Of the two, pins are more useful and precise as they do not pose the risk of being knocked out of their place.

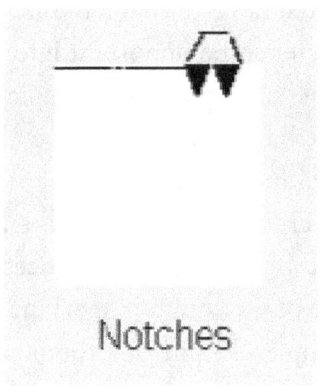

THIS WAY, it is much more convenient for a beginner. The pins must always be placed in the seam allowance. For cutting the pieces out, you can use a rotary cutter or a pair of scissors. For cutting purposes, scissors are far more precise and easier to handle.

As regards a rotary cutter, it may be a good option, but is quite difficult to use around the corners as it easily overshoots your mark; moreover, they are very sharp and might not be safe for a beginner. Scissors serve your purpose well until you get experienced.

Regarding the procedure of cutting around notches, there is a catch. In order to save time while printing the patterns, companies prefer to print the notch triangles toward the main part of the pattern piece. Never cut them toward the pattern piece, rather cut away from it. Notches have their utility in lining up the pieces when sewing them together.

Marking Pieces

Through the process, you'll come across numerous

projects where you'll have to mark the fabric pieces. While marking, you transfer some important information from the pattern piece to the cut fabric, for example as where to sew in darts, where the buttonholes are to be placed, where you must put the zipper and so on.

There are numerous ways to mark the fabric which you can choose depending on your preferences and the type of fabric in use. Some of the common marking elements are:

Pins—Most people use pins for the purpose of marking places such as start and stop for sewing and measurements. Care needs to be taken as some fabrics are left with tiny pinholes after you use them. Garments that stretch easily are the ones that can be used along with pins without any headache of pinholes. Therefore, I strongly recommend that you properly consider the placement of the pins and the fabric as well before going with this method. They are best to use when sewed in a seam line.

Tailor Tack

TAILOR TACKS—THE tailor tacking method uses threads for marking the fabric pieces. You can sew the thread through the fabric only or the pattern piece and the fabric. Having done this, cut the thread and pull off the pattern piece. You can see your mark in the exact right place.

Washable Ink Markers—Washable markers and those with disappearing ink come in numerous colors. You can choose any depending on your convenience and the color of the fabric.

For marking purposes, they are the easiest to use among all the methods available. Before using your pencil marker on the fabric, always try it on a rough piece of fabric just in order to ensure that it works fine.

The desirable qualities in such a marker include its long stay on the fabric; long enough to be useful such that it doesn't easily get rubbed or smeared off. At the same time, it must be easily removable with a fabric eraser.

Tracing Paper and Tracing Wheel—With this method, you have to place a tracing paper between the fabric and the pattern piece with the transfer color toward the fabric. Using the wheel, press down on the pattern marking which you wish to transfer. The color present on the paper will rub off onto the fabric.

Ribbing

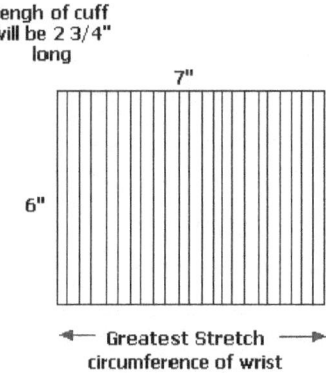

SEWING: GRANDMA'S SPECIAL TRICKS

MANY PEOPLE CONSIDER RIBBING as an indicator of the quality of finishing imparting to a finished garment. If a look inside the sleeve cuff ribbing shows you a seam running to the outer edge of the cuff, the garment has certainly been sewn up in haste.

Though it might save you some time, the finishing would be poor. I'm outlining here the procedure to attach a perfect ribbing but it must not be done in haste. All seams are ¼ inch. Add 1" to the measurement of your wrist or hip, whichever you are ribbing for. Cut a pattern in this size.

Now, cut out a piece of ribbing and make sure that the ribbing lines are as shown in the picture. The aim is to cut it in a way such that the stretch goes around the wrist. As per the diagram example, the wrist circumference is 6".

Now, fold the ribbing lengthwise with right sides together in the same direction as the ribbing lines. This will give you a tube of 6" long and 3.5" across. Sew a seam. When finished, fold your cuff in half right side out.

Now is the time when you can try your cuff. If the fitting is fine, continue with it, otherwise, make the necessary adjustments. Takedown the measurements. This unique cuff size can be used in all future projects.

Again, open the cuff such that it has the same shape as it will have on your wrist. Use pins to pin the cuff layers together in four places around the open circle. Place 4 pins around the open end of the sleeve, at equal distances. After this, your sleeve circumference would have been divided into 4 equal parts.

Now, place the cuff over the outside of the sleeve and ensure that the seams are matching. This way, the raw edges of the cuff will lie on top of the sleeve raw edges while the folded edge of the cuff would be lying toward the sleeve top as if it has been rolled up.

Sew the cuff to the sleeve, gently guiding the ribbing. Take care in ensuring that you sew only through one layer of the sleeve, otherwise you'll end up shutting off your sleeve completely.

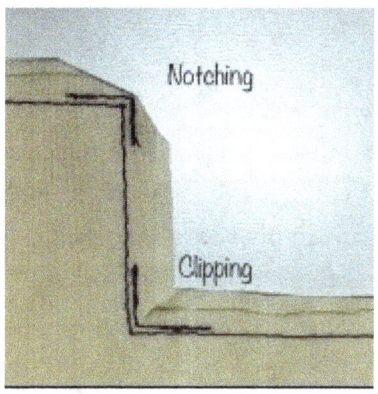

CLIPPING AND NOTCHING CURVES

Seam allowances are clipped and notched in order to mold them into a curve. This very thing makes the finished garment lie flat having nice flat seams and edges. If the edge of your fabric lies outside the curve of the seam allowance, you need a straight snip in the seam allowance in order to fix it. This process is known as clipping.

On the other hand, if the fabric edge curve lies inside the curve of the seam, a notch is cut into the seam allowance, which is a wedge shaped-cut, thereby removing the bulk in the seam allowance and allowing the seam allowance to lie flat. This is called notching.

FACING AND INTERFACING

WHEN YOU FINISH up with a garment, the edges are mostly in a raw form, and you need to finish them off in some way or the other. You can simply sew a seam binding to the edge or can hem a straight edge. But these will end up showing the stitches outside.

Moreover, with curved edges such as the one around an armhole, hemming would not simply work. For overcoming these issues, we have what is called facing. The facing is cut to the same shape as the edge and is sewn onto it.

Note that while sewing, the right sides must be together, and it is then turned to the inside of the garment (after seam allowances have been trimmed). To make the faced edge crispy, press it with a hot iron.

Interfacing is the process of providing more body to the facing by lining it a bit more. This provides extra firmness to the garment. Interfacing is generally used for providing stiffness to those garments which are to be used for lifting some heavyweight.

Different types of interfacings are available ranging from the fusible ones (iron-on) to sew-on ones. The fusible one is the most popular and highly recommended because of the ease with which it can be worked upon.

SEAM FINISHING

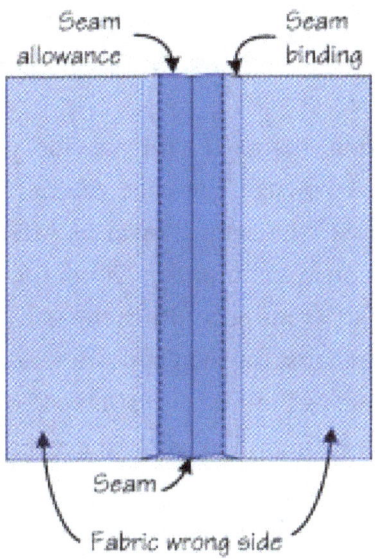

THE FIRST THREE of the mentioned techniques are used to finish the raw edges of the seam allowance after the seam has been stitched. The last two happen to encase the entire seam.

For bulkier seams such as double-sided pre-quilted fabric, the binding seam is the recommended technique. For delicate fabrics like sheer curtains that have the tendency to fray, French seam works best.

Pinking Shears—It is used for cutting a zigzag edge on the fabric such that it provides a finished look at it. Apart from giving it a finished look, pinking also prevents fraying.

SEWING: GRANDMA'S SPECIAL TRICKS

In order to impart some more protection against fraying, it's recommended that you add an extra line of stitching inside the pinked edge.

Zigzag Stitch—Zigzag stitch is provided to the fabric edging with the help of a sewing machine. To make perfect insulation against fraying, the zigzag pattern must be sewn very close to the edge such that the outer zigzag falls over the edge of the fabric.

Clean Finished Seam—It will provide your garment a nicely finished sewn edge. For this, you need to iron under ¼" along the edge of the seam allowance. After the first phase of ironing, iron once again under another ¼" and sew close to the edge. Apart from preventing the garment from fraying, it imparts the most finished appearance of all.

Binding Seams—Binding is stitched onto the seam allowance of the garment in exactly the same manner as it is done for a quilt or a placemat. It also covers the raw edges completely. It is a method used generally with heavy fabrics such as denims, jeans, etc., but there is no harm in using it for lightweight fabrics as well.

French Seams—In this method, the first seam holding the raw edges within itself is encased within another seam such that the second one provides backup and strength to the first one.

This method also provides nice finishing with no raw-edged appearing loose. First, stitch a seam with layers, the wrong side together. Now, fold back the fabric layers such that they become right sides together holding seam allowances in between. Again, stitch a new seam such that the edges of the first seam get totally encased within the new seam allowance.

Basting

Basting is done for the purpose of temporarily holding the fabric in place until you have provided your garment the final permanent stitching. For example, for holding a zipper, a seam can be basted temporarily.

Let's take an example: suppose you are working on a center back zipper; make it into two halves. Now, sew a center back seam starting from the bottom of the dressing and take it up to the point where you'll be installing the zipper.

The seam has been basted; it will hold the edges of the seam in place until you install the zipper. Once you are able to complete the final stitching, the basting will be removed, thereby putting an end to its temporary purpose.

Gathering

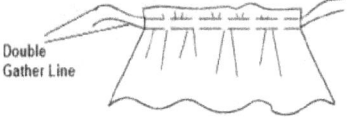

DONE EITHER by hand or by machine, gathering serves the purpose to ease in the fabric along the curves such as when sewn along the sleeve curves, or with curtains. The stitch here is quite similar to basting stitch—extra-long and straight. A plus point with gathering is its flexibility.

It can either be very subtle, just enough to ease the sleeve or can be completely fuller as in the case of a puffy sleeve or a skirt. The permanent stitch on the garment is placed right

SEWING: GRANDMA'S SPECIAL TRICKS

on top inside the gathering stitch, a little away from the fabric edge.

For full skirts or puffy sleeves, a proper gathering would require two lines of gathering stitches while the gathering used in gently easing in a sleeve would use only one line. In the former case, the second stitch would serve two important purposes: 1) firstly, it acts as a backup in case one of the threads breaks off and 2) secondly, it provides for a nice row of gatherers that are easy to control in spacing along with a much tighter, rounded appearance rather than a flat and folded look.

BUTTONHOLES

There are four basic steps for creating a buttonhole. However, different machines follow different sequences. Write-up here is just for illustration. Better go through your machine manual thoroughly before taking up the project for the buttonhole. The four steps are 1) zigzags across the upper end; 2) zigzags down one side; 3) zigzags across the lower end, and 4) zigzags up the other side.

Your machine will require you to select steps 1 through 4, mentioned above, by turning a dial. Mark the start and end of each buttonhole from the dial. However, if your machine is an advanced version, the whole process might be automated.

For making buttonholes, you'll need a buttonhole presser foot. You may note that for different fabrics, there may be a difference in density of the stitches when compared on the right and left sides of the buttonhole. By turning the dial on your machine, you may correct this anomaly.

Once you complete the sewing of the buttonhole, cut the center in one straight line. Please note that this cutting is not to be done until the buttonhole has been completed. This is because there is a probability that your buttonhole is of faulty size which can only be changed till the time central cutting has not been done.

Zippers

Basically, there are three types of zippers: centered zipper, lapped zipper and fly extension zipper. Before you start to put in the zipper, always baste the seam and keep pressing on. Low or medium heat is required for ironing the seams here. Use of zipper foot is recommended for all the steps and make sure that the basting is removed after you are done with installing the zipper.

CENTERED ZIPPER

First of all, baste the garment seam close using a 5/8" seam allowance. You'll be working on the inside of the garment. Keeping the zipper bottom away from yourself, extend the right seam allowance on the garment. This means that the garment is folded back out of the way thereby making you baste through the seam allowance only.

Most people don't make any

SEWING: GRANDMA'S SPECIAL TRICKS

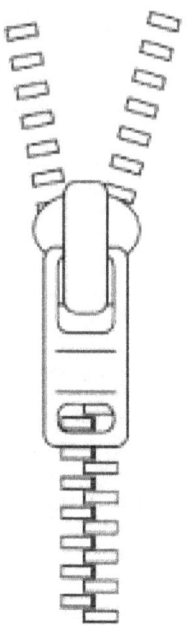

sewing on the garment at this juncture. This will also hold the zipper in thus making it easier for anyone to sew. Take the zipper tape and place it face down on the seam allowance, keeping the bottom stop on the marking point on the seam with the zipper coil lying directly on the seam. To make it even easier, you may like to pin the zipper in place before basting it.

Using a zipper foot, the machine bastes the right zipper tape in place on the right seam allowance, starting from the bottom of the zipper. Now, extend the left seam allowance and baste the left zipper tape in place.

You can also topstitch the zipper using a stitch that is slightly longer than a regular length. Work on the outside of the garment after spreading the garment flat. Use a pin to mark the bottom of the zipper. Starting at the seam, stitch up completely one side of the zipper. Repeat the process for the other side.

Lapped Zipper

For neck or skirt projects, the tab must be turned up; for side-dress applications, it must be put down. If your project includes a side-dress application, whip stitch the tapes together above the top stop in order to form a bar tack. Again, you will have to work on the inside of the garment.

Keeping the zipper bottom opening away from yourself, extend the right seam allowance. Put the closed zipper face down on the seam allowance such the bottom stop rests on the marking on the garment and the zipper coil and not on the seam. Baste the zipper into its place. There may occur the curving out of the stitching around the zipper.

You can now change to regular stitch length. Turning the zipper face up, form a fold in the seam allowance. Bring the fold very close to the coil without touching it. Stitch the fold to the zipper tape. In order to topstitch, make the garment lay flat. Make the zipper face turn down over the free seam allowance.

A pleat will form at the ends of the zipper opening. After securing this with pins, mark the bottom of the zipper with a pin on the outside of the garment. Starting from the seam, go on to stitch across the bottom and up one side of the zipper.

- Stay stitching
- Fussy cutting
- Use of bar tracks

MAINTENANCE

Maintaining your sewing machine is a simple task but requires precision. The steps to perform proper and adequate maintenance are as follows.

Dust removal is one of the main causes of jams and failures in sewing machines of any model. That's why the first thing you need to remove is dust.

To do this, you will need a brush and a soft bristle brush.

On many occasions, dust will accumulate and mix with oil residue, forming layers of lint that are difficult to remove. So, you must have patience, perseverance, and time on your hands to remove all this dirt.

Some essential parts from which you need to remove dust are:

- Needle holder
- Reel holder
- Spool boxes
- Presser's foot
- Inside the bobbin case

In addition, all parts we can access, and anywhere we notice dust, need to be well cleaned.

The inside, not just the outer parts, requires extensive maintenance. In addition, the inside of the sewing machine requires special treatment to ensure its operation.

To do this, we need to dismantle the presser foot and shuttle to reach inaccessible corners.

If the machine uses a metal bobbin, it is necessary to disassemble it and dust it off. You also need to remove the coil and check it for dust or other harmful residues.

After you've assured that there is no dust inside the most important parts of the machine, you will grease it. Greasing your sewing machine will allow the most important moving parts to run smoothly.

You should know that you can't apply oil to every part you can think of. The main piece of oil is the bobbin case.

You can also put oil on the shuttle and needle bars. This will be enough to ensure good mechanics of the moving parts.

It is not necessary to put a large amount of oil on the previously described parts. A drop on each part is more than enough.

Assemble and test. When you finish cleaning and oiling the sewing machine, it is recommended to test it immediately. This ensures that all the parts have been put in place correctly.

It also serves to let you feel the difference in performance to compare how it performed without proper maintenance and how it performs after care.

On the following pages, you can quickly and easily maintain your sewing machine at home.

. . .

SEWING: GRANDMA'S SPECIAL TRICKS

As you've noticed, sewing machine maintenance is relatively simple. However, the effectiveness can be reduced if the right materials and products are not used. Here is a list of recommended products and accessories for this process:

Nylon cleaning brush set: You need to use brushes with tiny, flexible bristles for deep and effective cleaning. That's why we recommend the ZOEON brush set.

The set contains eight brushes, each 23 centimeters long but with different styles on the tips.

These are ideal for reaching hard-to-reach places on sewing machines. In addition, they can be used to clean other appliances with similar features.

6-pc. Double-tipped sewing machine brushes: this brush incorporates a double-tipped structure in its design. This allows for cleaning with different shades of firmness.

The package consists of 5 brushes with the same features. When one of the brushes deteriorates, you will immediately have a replacement.

Sewing machine oil, 150 ml: Another essential product for the maintenance of sewing machines is oil. This allows lubrication of moving parts, extending the useful life of the machine components.

We recommend using Alfa sewing machine oil. Its 100 ml package is ideal for easy transport and use.

This oil provides a protective coating to sewing machine parts that prevents corrosion and dust from damaging components.

The cap is designed to add oil to key locations on the sewing machine easily.

5L Sewing Machine Oil: If you own a large business with many sewing machines, you will probably need a large amount of oil. For these cases, we recommend a 5-liter sewing machine oil.

It is an oil designed for the maintenance of domestic machines and for industrial models. It is resistant to high temperatures, forming a solid and effective film.

Can you fix your sewing machine if it encounters minor problems?

Here's a guide to fix the most common sewing problems faced by beginners:

Breaking needles

Always start with a new straight needle at the beginning of a new project. Be careful to avoid bent needles, as it can lead to needle breakage and eye entry! If your needles are breaking now, you know where to look first!

Non-threading

The root cause could be that the bobbin is not correctly concatenated through the thread guide. When you start sewing, make sure your thread guide is standing up.

Are your stitches opening at the ends?

Always be careful to stitch the edges double. To do this, pull the fabric back and forth after you finish the straight stitch and stitch back to the edge of the fabric, respectively.

Unprofessional sewing

For a perfect seam, never remove the fabric when done with a straight stitch. As you change direction, leave the needle rotated down on the fabric and continue sewing.

Undue noise when active

Something is jammed in your machine. De-assemble and clean the lint from the machine with a brush.

SEWING: GRANDMA'S SPECIAL TRICKS

GRANDMA'S SEWING special tips

Never leave the thread guide down when you start sewing; otherwise, your needle will slip out the moment you start sewing.

Always start by checking your stitches on a rough fabric patch before beginning on a brand-new fabric.

Avoid using oddly shaped needles, as there's a chance they'll ruin your eyes and your work irreparably!

If you notice skipped stitches, your needle is rotten!

Always keep a patch of the fabric and 2 inches of thread from the material you are working on as a miniature record of your results.

If you notice strange noises coming from your sewing machine, unplug it immediately and call the manufacturer.

Just like your computer, there is a manual restart to troubleshoot your sewing machine. Re-threading and rewinding the bobbins from square one will help you remove mild jams.

STEP-BY-STEP SEWING PROJECTS (27 PROJECTS)

Simple Tote Bag
Materials:

- 1/3" yard of felt fabric or Aida cloth (If your child is a little older, you may use strong cotton fabrics
- Buttons, beads, felt fabric (for designs)
- Double-sided tape
- Ready-made patches
- Colorful embroidery threads
- Magnetic buttons
- 1 – 6"x12" rectangle-shaped fabric
- 4 – 1"x10" rectangle-shaped fabric (for the handle/strap)

Directions:

1. Thread the needle.
2. Make ½" fold on the 6" sides of the large

SEWING: GRANDMA'S SPECIAL TRICKS

rectangular fabric. Design the fabric using beads or ready-made patches. Sew them on the right side. Do not place any decoration in the middle of the rectangle or the edges of the fabric.
3. Fold the large rectangular fabric lengthwise to make a 6" square. The right side should be outside.
4. Using double-sided tape, secure the two sides. Leave the top portion open.
5. Sew the side of the square using the overstitch. Make small stitches. Once finished, you now have the base of the tote bag.
6. For the handle, join two of the fabrics. Sew all the sides using the running stitch. You may sew a ribbon over it as a design. Try to make the stitches aligned. Do the same to the other handle.
7. Attach the handle to the bag. One on each side. Position the ends of the handle to the bag. Secure using the tape. Top one of the edges with a button. Sew the button, the handle and one side of the bag together.
8. Repeat the step until the two handles are secured. Add more buttons to the handle to make it more secure.
9. You may also add magnetic buttons to the opening so you can close the bag when you need to.

This tote bag can be used as your child's lunch bag, too.
Friendly Cushions
Materials:

- 6 – 7"x7" pre-cut felt paper

- Scrap felt papers of different colors (black and white are a must)
- Pillow stuffing
- Embroidery threads
- Doll's eyes or bird's eyes buttons (1" in size)
- Double-sided tapes
- Papers and pencil
- Draw faces on a piece of paper.
- Using the face as a reference, make a pattern of the parts of the faces.

Directions:

1. Using the patterns, cut out the parts of the faces using felt fabrics.
2. Take one of the pre-cut felt fabrics. Arrange one of the faces on the right side of the fabric. Using the double-sided tape, secure the faces to the fabric.
3. Thread the needle.
4. Permanently secure the faces to the fabric by using a running stitch or backstitch. Sew the eye buttons.
5. Place the designed fabric over another pre-cut felt fabric. The right side should be on the inside.
6. Sew all the sides of the layers to make a pillow casing. Leave a small opening. Invert the casing to expose the right side.
7. Stuff the casing using cotton or other stuffing materials.
8. Close the opening.
9. Do the same with the other set of pre-cut fabrics, so you will have three friendly cushions.

SEWING: GRANDMA'S SPECIAL TRICKS

Variety: If using faces is hard for your child, just use basic shapes or letters as designs. You may also use other pre-cut shapes for the base.

Pillows, Pillow Cases and Comforters

Materials:

- 1 meter of cotton fabric (You may also use ½ meter of solid colored fabric and printed fabric)
- Yardstick
- Water-based markers
- Batting material for the bedding (1/4" thick)
- Cotton stuffing
- Pins

Directions:
For The Comforter:

1. Measure two 24"x32" of fabrics. Let her mark the fabric using the water-based markers instead of the tailor chalk.
2. Stack the two fabrics together. If using two different textiles, make sure the right side of the printed fabric should be on the inside.
3. Draw a straight line on all sides of the fabrics, 1 inch away from the edges.
4. Secure the fabrics together using pins.
5. Using the line as a guide, sew the edges of the fabrics. Straight stitch or triple stretch stitch may be used for this. Leave at least a 6" opening in one of the sides.
6. Invert the fabrics to show the right side.

7. Measure the actual size of the sewn comforter. Cut the basting in the same measurement as the actual size of the comforter.
8. Insert the basting inside the comforter. Flatten it neatly inside. Close the opening by hand stitching.
9. Using a water-based marker, mark a smaller rectangle in the center of the comforter.
10. Using the lines as a guide, sew the straight lines using the machine. Use triple stretch stitch and a different color of thread. This will serve as a design. If your child prefers, you can let her use wavy or diagonal lines across the comforter.
11. Note: These steps of making a comforter may also be used as a reference for basic quilting.

For The Pillow:

1. Measure and cut two 8"x12" of fabric. Using the same fabrics is preferred.
2. Stack two fabrics together. Place a straight line on each side, 1" away from the edges.
3. Using the line as a guide, sew the edges using the straight stitch or triple stretch stitch. Leave a small opening, about 3 inches.
4. Stuff the pillow to the desired thickness. If it is meant for the baby, 2" thickness may be enough.
5. Close the opening by hand sewing.
6. Make another pillow using the same steps.

For The Pillowcase:

SEWING: GRANDMA'S SPECIAL TRICKS

1. Measure and cut two 11"x15" of fabric.
2. Draw a line on the top part of the fabric, 1" from the edge. Using the line as a guide, fold the fabric toward the wrong side to make a 1" hem. Sew the hem using the straight stitch or the triple stretch stitch.
3. Stack 2 fabrics together. The wrong side should be on the outside. Draw straight lines on the sides of the fabric, 1" from the edge. Do not draw a line on the sewn seam.
4. Using the lines as guides, sew the edges using a straight stitch.
5. Invert the fabric. You now have a pillowcase for your pillow.
6. Make another pillowcase using the same steps.

The "Me" Pillow
Materials:

- 1 meter of fabric (you may add a few more if your child is bigger)
- Stuffing

Directions:

1. Stack two layers of fabric. The right side should be on the inside.
2. Let her lie on the fabric. Using tailor chalk or water-based marker, trace her body on the fabric. Add 2" to the edges for the hems. From here, let her do the work.

3. Cut the shape.
4. Sew the edges of the doll. Leave an opening on the foot. About 3 to 4" wide.
5. Reverse the doll casing to show the right side.
6. Stuff the doll. You may have to use the meter stick to push the stuffing to the hands and head.
7. Close the opening. Now, she has her "Me" doll. You may decorate the doll using ready-made patches. Or you could attach a doll's or bird's eyes on the head. You may also let it wear some of her clothes.

Sleeveless Sundress for Her Doll
Materials:

- 1/3 yard printed cotton textile
- Half yard of thin garter
- Ribbons
- Tape Measure

Directions:

1. Take the measurements of the chest, waist, the distance between the chest and the waist and the desired length of the dress. You may show your child how to take measurements using the tape measure.
2. Make the pattern and cut the fabric. For this sundress, the pattern will be a simple trapezoid. The upper portion should be the shorter side. For the chest, add 2" to the actual measurement of the chest. For the waist, add 4" and for the skirt add 6"

SEWING: GRANDMA'S SPECIAL TRICKS

or 8". For the length of the dress, add 2" at the bottom (You may have to guide your child in creating the pattern).
3. Prepare two of the trapezoid-shaped fabric.
4. Cut the garter. The length should be 1cm shorter than the measurement of the chest.
5. Make a 1" fold on the top and bottom of the trapezoid-shaped fabric. Fold toward the wrong side. For this project, use pins to secure the fabric for sewing. Do the same to the other fabric. Use backstitch or running stitch.
6. Join the two trapezoid-shaped fabrics. The right side should be hidden. Sew the sides of the skirt.
7. On the chest, insert the garter inside the top seam. You can do this by tying the garter to a hairpin and push the hairpin inside the seam. Join the top portions using the garter. Untie the garter and stitch the end together by using the overstitch.
8. Sew the sides of the dress completely. The dress may look like a long skirt. The chest part will also appear a little ruffled.
9. Fit the dress to the doll. If the chest part fits the doll and it does not fall down, then the dress is done. If the chest part is loose, then you may have to use the ribbon to make the strap.

You may use the ribbon as a belt or just leave the dress flowing.

Old Clothes Cushions
Materials:

- Old Shirts or Pants

- Stuffing

Directions:

1. Reverse the shirt or the pants so that the right side will be on the inside.
2. Sew the neck opening, the arms opening using a triple stretch stitch or straight stitch.
3. Sew the body opening, too, but leave a few inches open. Reverse the shirts to show the right side.
4. Place the pillow stuffing inside the shirt and close the opening.

Used Clothes Lunch and Tote Bags
Materials:

- Old overall jumper
- Old undershirt for boys

Directions:

1. Cut the legs of the overall jumper.
2. Reverse the overall.
3. Sew the opening on the leg part.
4. Invert it to show the right side.
5. Done. You now have an overall lunch bag. The armholes will serve as the handle.

For the Tote Bag:

1. Reverse the undershirt.
2. Sew the bottom part.

3. Reverse the shirt again. You now have a tote bag. Again, the armholes will serve as the handle.

Headbands
Materials:

- 4"x20" strip of fabric (printed fabrics are preferred)
- Ribbons
- Ready-made patches (optional)

Directions:

1. Fold the fabric in half, crosswise. The right side should be on the inside.
2. Place a straight line on the two long sides of the fabric, ½" away from the edge. Use a water-based marker.
3. Sew the fabric, using the line as a guide. Leave one of the ends of the strip open.
4. Invert the sewn fabric. You may use a ruler to help you push one end of the strip to the open end.
5. Flatten the fabric. Fold ½" of the open end to the inside. This is to hide the hems of the fabric.
6. Close the open end using the machine.
7. Draw another line on each side of the sewn fabric, ¼" from the edge.
8. Sew the lines using the straight stitch or the triple stretch stitch. If you want to place a simple design on the band, use the zigzag stitch. You may also sew a strip of thin ribbon on the middle of the

band or ready-made patches on the top side of the headband.
9. If the headband is a little short, you can use a 1" size ribbon as an extender.

Loop T-Shirt Dress
Materials:

- 1 shirt that fits you perfectly
- 1 larger shirt that you can cut
- Scissors
- Thread
- Needles

Directions:

1. First, put the smaller shirt on top of the large one up until the neckline then use the said neckline as a marking for where you'll cut the cloth.
2. Cut until you make holes for sleeves and shoulders and belled-out sides and go on until you see the large shirt's hem.
3. With the pieces that you have cut off, cut two rectangular pieces that you'll later use to make loops.
4. Fold the rectangular pieces lengthwise, in half, and make sure that the right sides are close together. Sew the edges.
5. Now, turn the fabric right side out.
6. Take the rectangular pieces together and loop them, like you are looping some ribbons or knots.

SEWING: GRANDMA'S SPECIAL TRICKS

This will give the shirt some form. Use basting stitches to hold the loops in place.
7. Pin front and back pieces together before sewing. Make sure to leave ¼ inch of space. If you want something shorter, cut at least 3 inches from the hem and you're set.
8. Enjoy your new dress!

Elastic Headband
Materials:

- 3"x20" strip of fabric (printed fabrics are preferred; the size may vary depending on the size of the child's head)
- 1" elastic band

Directions:

1. Measure the size of your head using the tape measure. The length of the fabric should be your size of head plus 6 inches.
2. Fold the fabric crosswise to make it 1½ inch wide. Make sure that the right side is on the inside. Secure it with a pin or baste it using wide running stitches. Join them permanently using the triple stretch stitch or the straight stitch.
3. Reverse the fabric to show the right side. You can do this by using a ruler to push one end to the other end.
4. Cut the elastic band. The length of the band should be the size of your head minus 1 inch.
5. Attach the band on a safety pin. Insert the safety

pin into the fabric and pull the elastic band to the other end. Make sure that the other end of the band does not enter the fabric.
6. Join the two ends of the elastic band. Sew it using the zigzag stitch or the triple stretch stitch.
7. Fold the ends of the fabric toward the wrong side. Sew the two ends together by hand or by machine.
8. Adjust the pleats of the headband. Wear them.

Tip: You can also use the steps of the elastic headband to make a ponytail band. Just shorten the length of the fabric to 8" and the elastic band to 4". Use a thinner elastic band, too.

Kiddie Apron

Materials:

- ½ meter of fabric
- Tape measure
- Pattern paper (optional)
- Double-sided tape
- Buttons (optional)

Directions:

1. Take the measurement of the desired length of the apron. Add 2 more inches for the hemstitching.
2. Take the measurement of the desired width of the upper part of the apron. The measurement is usually half of the chest measurement. Just add 2 more inches for the hemstitching.
3. Take the measurement of the desired width of the skirt of the apron. The measurement is usually half

SEWING: GRANDMA'S SPECIAL TRICKS

of the hip measurement. Add 2 more inches for the hemstitching.
4. Take the measurement of the distance between the chest and the waist/hip.
5. On the pattern paper, draw a trapezoid. The top part of the trapezoid should be the chest part and the bottom part should be the skirt part.
6. Cut the pattern and use it to cut the fabric.
7. *This step can be omitted. You may directly draw the shape on the fabric using water-based markers.
8. Fold 1 inch to each side of the cut fabric. Secure the hem using pins or double-sided tape. Make sure to fold the hem toward the wrong side.
9. Stitch all the hems. Now, you have the base of the apron.
10. Cut 4 – 2"x10" strips of fabric. Fold 1 strip crosswise to make it 1"x10". Make sure that the right side is hidden. Secure with pins if needed.
11. Sew the sides of the strip, leaving one of the ends open. Reverse the fabric.
12. Fold the open end toward the inside and close it either by hand sewing or by using the machine. Repeat steps 8 and 9 until you had made 4 strips.
13. Sew two of the strips on each corner of the upper part of the apron. You may sew it directly through the machine, but attach it from the wrong side of the apron. Or, you may attach it on the right side using two buttons (Just like what was done in the tote bag in Chapter 3). This will serve as the neck strap of the apron.
14. Sew two of the strips on the side of the apron, a

few inches below the waist area. Sew it on the wrong side of the apron. This will serve as the belt.

Kiddie Pot Holders
Materials:

- 1/3 meter of cotton fabric
- 1/3 meter of muslin fabric
- Batting material (anti-heat)
- Pins

Directions:

1. Make the hand patterns. There should be a left and a right-hand pattern.
2. Trace your hands and wrists. Do not trace each of your fingers. Just trace the thumb. Then trace the four fingers together. Retrace the drawn hands to make them bigger. About 2" bigger.
3. Cut the patterns and place them over the fabric.
4. Cut 3 pieces of the left-hand pattern (2 pieces using the printed fabric and 1 piece using the muslin). Do the same using the right-hand pattern.
5. Trace the same patterns to the batting material. Make a pair of hands.
6. Stack 2 pieces of the printed fabric, 1 batting material and 1 muslin fabric. All should be on the right side. Sew the edges of the hand.
7. Fold ½ inch hem on the wrist end. Secure with pins. Sew the hem.
8. You may sew straight lines on the hands to secure the batting or create a design pattern on the hand.

SEWING: GRANDMA'S SPECIAL TRICKS

9. Repeat steps 6, 7 and 8 using the other three pieces of fabrics and the batting material for the other hand.
10. Join the left and the right hand. The right side should be facing each other.
11. Stitch the hands together. Leave the wrist part open. Now, you have your own kiddie pot holder.

Tip: This potholder can also be used as a winter mitten. Just change the cotton fabric into a knitted fabric and make the batting material thinner. Also, make the hand pattern size 1" smaller. Just follow the same steps.

Elastic Waist Skirt

Materials:

- ½ meter printed fabric
- Tape measure
- 1" size garter or elastic band

Directions:

1. Take the measurement of your waist. Double it. This will be the width of the fabric you should use for the skirt.
2. Take the measurement of the desired length of the skirt. Add 2 inches to the length.
3. Cut a rectangle using the dimension mentioned above.
4. Fold a 1½ inch hemline on one side of the width of the fabric. Sew it but leave the ends open and

the middle hollow. This will serve as the waist part.
5. Fold a ½" hemline on the other edge of the fabric. Sew it first using a straight stitch. Then, run a zigzag stitch over the straight stitch. This will create a cleaner hem.
6. You may attach edging designs or ribbons to the fabric if you desire.
7. Cut the garter or the elastic band. The measurement should be equal to your waist minus 1 inch.
8. Insert the elastic band on the hollow hem. To do this, attach one end of the elastic band to a safety pin. Insert the pin to the hem and push it toward the other end. Gather the fabric toward the middle of the band as you push the band to the end. Make sure that the other end of the band does not enter the hem.
9. Join the two ends of the elastic band and sew them together.
10. Join the two ends of the fabric and sew them together. Make sure that the right side is on the inside.
11. Reverse the skirt and arrange the pleats of the belt part. Your skirt is complete.

Tip: You may add a pocket to your skirt, too. Just cut a 5" x5" fabric. If you want a "U" shape pocket, just cut it into that shape. Clean the edges by sewing a ½" hem on each side.

Attach this pocket to the fabric during step 5. Just sew the sides and bottom part of the pocket. Make sure to sew it on the right side of the skirt.

Afghan

Materials:

- 4 skeins worsted weight yarn, or 900-1,000 yards. 100% acrylic or an acrylic-nylon blend works well.
- Size 10 circular needle, with a 20" cord

Directions:

1. Cast on 144 stitches, but do not join in the round. Use the circular needle to support the weight.
2. Repeat for the following four rows:

Row One: Knit one, purl one, alternating across.
Row Two: Knit one, purl one, alternating across.
Row Three: Purl one, knit one, alternating across.
Row Four: Purl one, knit one, alternating across.

1. Join new skeins of yarn as they are needed until you are close to the end. Cast off. Weave in the ends using a crochet hook or needle. Trim the tails with sharp scissors when needed.

Customizing the Pattern:

There are two ways that you can easily customize the pattern. One is to make it longer and more squared by simply doubling the amount of yarn used. You can also change the types of yarn used to create a different feel and look for the finished product. It makes it easy to customize them for seasonal use or as gifts.

Purse

Materials:

- 2 skeins of desired color medium weight cotton or cotton-wool blend yarn. It will take roughly 140 yards total.
- 1 pair size 8 knitting needles
- Scissors
- Yarn needle
- 2 size 8 double-pointed needles or an I-cord maker

The finished product is about 8" wide and 20" long in its unfolded form. The actual purse will be 8" wide, 8" long and a 4" closure flap.

Directions:

1. Using the single-pointed needles cast on 35 stitches.
2. Knit in Fleck Stitch for 20 inches.

Row 1: Knit the entire row.
Row 2: Purl the entire row.
Row 3: Knit 1, purl 1, knit 1. Repeat across the width.
Row 4: Purl the entire row.
Repeat for the remaining 20".

1. Cast off. Fold the rectangle so that the front is 8 inches and there is a 4" flap at the back that folds over the front.
2. Sew side seams together securely.
3. Create the strap by using double-pointed needles. Cast on 4 stitches and work 30 inches of I-cord, or use an I-cord maker.

SEWING: GRANDMA'S SPECIAL TRICKS

4. Attach the strap by stitching it securely to the inside of the purse.

Customizing the Pattern:
To keep items from pushing through the knitted material, you can line the inside with a complimentary colored fabric.

Rectangular Table Cloth

Materials:

- 2x2 yards of fabric or more, depending on the size of your table
- Tailor's chalk
- Measurement tape
- Ruler

What You Will Learn:

- Double-fold hem
- Measuring and cutting

Directions:

1. First, think about how long you want your tablecloth to be. Place the fabric on the table to get a feel. Then measure from the raw edge to the point where you want your tablecloth to start.
2. Place the fabric on an even surface and trace the measurements accordingly, then cut.

Double-Fold Seam:

1. Fold and press the raw edges at 1", then fold one

more time and press again. This procedure will ensure nice, crisp edges.
2. Sew a straight stitch about 1/8" away from the inner edge.
3. Cut out a small square on each corner. This prevents the fabric from getting bulky at the corners as you are about to overlap the edges.
4. Reaching your first corner, hold the fabric pressed. To navigate the corner, lift the presser foot and rotate the piece at a 45° angle until you are aligned with the next hem.
5. Finish up sewing all four hems. You are done!

Fabric Storage Box
Materials:

- 2 squares of fabric
- 1 square of interfacing
- Tailor's chalk
- Ruler

What You Will Learn:
Fusing interfacing.
Directions:

1. Cut out two equal squares of fabric. You can even use fabric scraps, sew them together and trim to a square. The fabric below measures 12"x12".
2. Take one square and place the interfacing on top, with the shiny part facing the fabric. For best results, read the directions of your interfacing.

Some interfacings require a higher fusing temperature than others.
3. Once you have fused the pieces together, trim off any excess interfacing.
4. Place the squares on top of each other, right sides facing. Sew together with a ¼" seam allowance. Leave an opening on one side, so you can turn the piece inside out later on. Use a backstitch on each end of the stitch so the seam doesn't open up as you work with the piece.
5. Snip off a tiny piece at each corner, making sure not to cut off the actual stitch. Then grab the corners and pull them through the opening.
6. Sew the opening shut with a topstitch.
7. Iron the piece if needed, then fold it in half. Measure the short side and make a marking at the center. Then mark the same distance on the long folded edge.
8. For example, if your short edge is 6", then you make a marking at 3". Moving on to the long folded edge, mark 3" from the outer corner. Unite the two points with tailor's chalk.
9. Sew a straight stitch on the marked line.
10. Once done, place the right edge on the adjacent and sew another straight stitch.
11. Repeat this method with the remaining two edges.
12. Turn the piece inside out. You can leave the box as it is or you can hand-stitch the four flaps into place, using a button on each outer corner.

Multi-Purpose Tool Organizer
Directions:

- 3 fabric rectangles
- 1 fusible interfacing
- Tailor's chalk
- Measurement tape
- Attaching ribbon
- Top-stitching compartments

Directions:

1. Determine the size of your project by using an item as a guideline. The item should be placed so as to have enough space around it. Cut out the lining, the interfacing and the main fabric to the same size.
2. Fuse the interfacing to either the lining or the main fabric. Since the main fabric was already thick enough, I decided to enforce the lining instead.
3. With your item, make a rough measurement for the pocket. Note that it should be twice the size so it can be folded in half. This will later create a crisp and clean edge.
4. Once you have determined the size of the pocket, line up the fabric inside out and stitch with ¼" seam allowance. Then turn the pocket inside out and press with the seam running through the middle of the piece. This will ensure nice and even compartments.
5. Place the pressed pocket onto the lining fabric and pin. You want to pin the piece with the inner seam running down. Sew the two pieces together to

create one wide pocket. Make a backstitch at each end to secure.
6. It is time to take out all your tools and place them on the project. This way, you can decide how wide or narrow you need your compartments to be. In the case of the makeup brushes, the compartments are of similar width. In other cases, the compartments can vary from narrow to wide.
7. Mark the compartments with tailor's chalk and a ruler, then topstitch. To prevent the seams from opening up later on, backstitch every time you reach the upper edge.
8. Place the main fabric onto the compartments, right sides facing and pin together.
9. Take a matching ribbon and cut a strip that is twice the width of your project. You will be able to trim off the excess later.
10. If you are working with a synthetic ribbon, carefully burn the ends with a candle to prevent fraying.
11. Fold the ribbon in half and make a loose knot. Then slide the ribbon in between the fabrics, with a little fold sticking out.
12. Sew the pieces together, leaving an opening at the bottom. Through this opening, you will be able to turn the project inside out.
13. Snip off the corners without cutting through the seam. Then turn the project inside out and press. Close the bottom opening with a seam.

Multi-Purpose Bag
Materials:

- 2 rectangles of fabric
- 1 rectangle of interfacing or batting
- Tailor's chalk
- Measurement tape
- Ruler
- Zipper
- Zipper foot (optional)
- 6 strips of fabric for Honk Kong seam

What's New:

- Attaching a zipper
- Honk Kong seam

Directions:

1. Although this bag can be done in any size, one rule is that you will need a rectangle shape. In the project below, the measurements are 20"x15".
2. Cut the main fabric, the lining and the interfacing into equally large rectangles. Fuse the interfacing on the lining or the main fabric.
3. Pin the zipper with its right side facing the right side of the main fabric. Then pin the lining onto the fabric, right sides facing. The zipper should be sandwiched between the two fabrics. Sew together with a straight stitch.
4. A zipper foot gives a nicer and more professional look. It has two sides where it can be attached to the machine, making it easier to stitch as close to the zipper as possible. If you don't have a zipper

SEWING: GRANDMA'S SPECIAL TRICKS

foot, don't worry, just use a regular foot and set your machine to a left side stitch.
5. Sew all three layers together—the lining, the zipper and the main fabric.
6. As you sew, you will notice that the slider will get in your way. Lift up the presser foot with the needle down, pull the slider a few inches down, then lower the foot and continue sewing.
7. Once you catch up with the slider again, lift the presser foot and pull it back up.
8. Carefully iron along the zipper. Do not iron on top of the zipper if it's made of plastic.
9. Trim the zipper if it's too long, then pin the end so the slider doesn't detach from the teeth by accident.
10. Take the main fabric and pin it on the empty side of the zipper.
11. Fold the lining inwards. Again, the zipper will be sandwiched between the right sides of the fabrics. Sew the three pieces together.
12. Once you have sewn both sides of the zipper, open up the piece. Notice that the wrong sides are facing out and the right sides are facing in.
13. Search for the zipper and open it up, being careful not to fully open through the trimmed edge.
14. Pull out the lining through the opening.
15. Layout your piece with the zipper in the center. Trim off the frays if necessary.
16. Sew the two raw edges on each side with a straight stitch and ¼" seam allowance.
17. On each corner, find the center between the outer edge and the zipper. Mark that distance on the

long-folded edge, too. Mark a small square on each corner. Then cut out the corners.
18. Carefully open each corner one at a time. Pull on the corners until their raw edges match. Seal the opening with a straight stitch of 1/8" seam allowance. Repeat on every corner.
19. Because you want your bag to be as sturdy as possible, a Hong Kong seam is a good choice for finishing the edges. For this, cut out 6 strips of fabric, each 1¼" wide. The length depends on the bag. Two pieces should correspond to the horizontal edges (where the zipper starts and ends) and four strips will be used for each corner. Cut a bit longer than your measurement.
20. Start with the horizontal edges. Sew the strip on the bag, right sides facing. Pull the strip up, then turn the bag, fold the strip in half and secure with pins if needed. Repeat on the other side.
21. Moving on to the four remaining corner strips, repeat the process, but this time you need to create nice, clean ends. You can do so by folding the strip on each end before sewing it.
22. Turn the bag inside out. Decide what length you want your straps to be, then add another inch for the seam allowance.
23. For this model, you can use the two fabrics as shown below. The lining fabric is wider than the main fabric, so it creates nice clean borders.
24. Double fold the bottom fabric on top of the main fabric. Then topstitch the straps.
25. Stitch the straps on the bag, then lift up the straps and pin.

26. Topstitch the straps all the way to the upper edge of the bag.

Scarf

Materials:

- Yarn: Total of 125 yards, but dispersed over 2 different strands
- 2 size 50 needles
- Scissors
- Yarn needle size 8, or crochet hook of comparable size
- The size of the completed scarf will be approximately 7" by 60".

Directions:

1. Grip all four strands of the yarn together and cast on 10 stitches.
2. Knit in garter stitch for the entire 60", or until it is at your desired length.
3. Cast off, but keep it loose.
4. Cut the yarn with the scissors and weave in the ends.
5. Customize the pattern:
6. Colors are very easy to customize, but you can also change the type of yarn for a different feel. Making scarves is a great last-minute gift option.

Wraps

- 1,000 yards total of medium weight cotton blend yarn
- 1 pair size 7 knitting needles
- Scissors
- Yarn needle

The finished wrap will be approximately 20" wide and 60" long.

Directions:

1. Cast on 120 stitches.
2. Knit in knit 2, purl 2 and continue until it is of the desired length.
3. Cast off.
4. Cut yarn with scissors and weave in the ends.
5. Customize the pattern:
6. Create a different look by using a different fiber yarn or a switch in colors. You can create a special look for your entire wardrobe.

Round Neck Rectangular T-Shirt
Materials:

- 1.5x1.5 yards of knit jersey fabric
- Measurement tape
- Ruler
- Curve ruler
- Tailor's chalk
- Twin needle (optional)

What's New:

SEWING: GRANDMA'S SPECIAL TRICKS

- Cutting bias from fabric
- Installing a round neckline

Directions:

1. With a measuring tape, measure the length from one shoulder to the other. You can also measure the shoulder length from a T-shirt in your wardrobe.
2. Once you have the measurement, add 14" to include the seam allowance and the sleeve length. This number will be the width of the piece.
3. Next, measure the length from your shoulder down to the hip. Add another 1 ½" to the number for seam allowance. This will be the length of the piece.
4. Note: If you want your project to be longer, i.e. covering your glutes, just add as many inches as you need to the length.
5. Now fold your fabric in half and trace the measurements.
6. For optimal results, the knitting direction of the fabric should be vertical (running downwards).
7. Now, you should have two rectangles. As they lay straight on top of each other, fold them in half, with the folded edge running downwards. From the corner of the folded edge, measure 2" toward the center top. Then measure 1" down from the corner. Connect the two points with a curved line, either free-handed or using a curve ruler. Then cut the corner out through all four layers of fabric.
8. Now set aside one fabric rectangle. This will be the

back piece. As the front piece needs to have a deeper cut, we need to widen the neckline on the front piece. To do so, mark and cut 1" down.
9. Place the piece's right sides facing and pin the upper raw edges together. Sew with a zigzag stitch.
10. Take the vertical raw edges and make a double fold, first by folding ½", then another ½". Pin into place and sew with a straight stitch. Repeat the process for the bottom horizontal edges.

Note: You can choose to make a simple one-time fold hem if you consider the double fold hem to be too bulky. It depends on the thickness of your fabric.

Repeat the process on the lower raw edges.

Tip: Do not stretch or stress the fabric while you are stitching.

One more tip: You can pinch the corners of the fabric to avoid a bulky hem.

Optional: This is the time to use your twin needle if you wish.

1. Measure the neckline with a measurement tape, then add 1 ½" to that number.
2. From the remaining fabric, cut a bias strip 1 ½" wide. The bias is the diagonal direction, which is the most stretchable part of the fabric. Cutting a bias strip will ensure that the neckline stays flat on the chest, giving it a neat look.
3. Fold the bias strip in half and press. Pin the center of the bias strip to the center front of the garment, right sides facing. Work your way all along the raw edge of the neckline.

SEWING: GRANDMA'S SPECIAL TRICKS

4. Sew together with a zigzag stitch.
5. To finish up the neckline, turn the loose ends of the bias strips so that their right sides are facing each other. Seal them together with a straight stitch.
6. Pull each end in opposite directions and tuck the seam into the strip. Finish the neckline by closing with a zigzag stitch.
7. Now we are going to sew the last two seams. For this, measure your bust and add another 2-3" depending on how loose you want the garment to be. From there, go down another 2" and start tracing a diagonal line all the way to the outer corners of the garment.
8. Topstitch the diagonal lines. Make a t-shaped stitch at each upper end to secure the stitch.
9. The following projects won't be checked due to excess in the word count:

Neck Tight T-Shirt
Materials

- 1.5 x 1.5 yards of fabric
- Tailor's chalk
- Measurement tape
- Ruler
- Twin needle
- Tracing paper

What's new:

- V-neck technique
- Tracing a sleeve pattern
- Attaching short sleeves
- Hemming with twin needle

Directions

1. Fold your fabric in half, with the knit running downwards, then fold one more time to get 4 layers of fabric.
2. Measure yourself from shoulder to shoulder, then divide the number by 2 and add ½" for seam allowance.
3. For example, if your shoulder-to-shoulder measurement is 15", you divide it by 2, making it 7 ½". Add ½" for seam allowance and you get 8".
4. Trace this measurement horizontally on the fabric.
5. Next, measure the distance between shoulder and armpit. In the demonstration below, it is 6".
6. Mark down from the shoulder line.
7. Measure your bust, then add another 1-3" if you want to it to be a loose fit, then divide the number by 4 and add ½" for seam allowance.
8. Example:
9. Bust measurement 32 / 4 = 8
10. Adding a loose fit 8 + 1 = 9
11. Adding seam allowance 9 + ½ = 9 ½
12. Trace the measurement horizontally along the last marking.

13. Connect the shoulder with the bust using a curve ruler. This will be the armhole.
14. Lastly, measure the length from your shoulder to your hips, then add 2" for seam allowance and the hem. This will determine the length of your t-shirt. As you go tracing down, you can either trace a straight line, or go with a curved line for a tighter fit.
15. Trace and cut the neckline, 1 ½" deep and 3" long.
16. Set the first piece aside. This will be the back piece. For the front, lay the remaining piece flat, measure 6" down from the neckline, then unite with the upper corner of the neckline using a straight line. For the arm, trace and cut ½" into the armhole.
17. Lay the pieces together right sides facing, then sew the shoulder edges using a zigzag stitch.
18. For the sleeve, you will need three measurements: the armhole, the sleeve length and the sleeve width.
19. The armhole is, as measured before, the distance between your shoulder and under your armpit.
20. The sleeve length is how long you want your sleeve to be. To determine this, just use the measurement tape and let it fall along your arm.
21. The sleeve width is the circumference at the widest point of your arm.
22. Take a piece of tracing paper and fold it in half. At the folded edge, measure the sleeve length and add 1" for allowance.
23. From there, mark 3 ½". On that line, trace the measurement of your armhole.
24. For the sleeve width, measure your arm

circumference at its widest point, then divide by 2 and add ½" seam allowance (SA).
25. Trace a tilted line toward the outer edge of the paper, thus connecting the arm width.
26. Connect the tip of the armhole to the top of the sleeve with a curved line. For this, you can use a curve ruler.
27. Cut out the paper. On one side, cut ½" into the curved line. This will mark the front of the sleeve.
28. Pin the sleeves together, remembering to match the front of the sleeve with the front piece of the garment and the back of the sleeve with the back of the garment. Sew together with a zigzag stitch and ½" seam allowance.
29. Now sew the sides of the garment with a zigzag stitch and ½" seam allowance.
30. Turn the garment inside out, measure the total length of the neckline and add another 1 ½". Cut a bias strip 2 ½" wide and as long as your measurement suggests.
31. Fold the strip, right sides facing, and from the middle, mark 1" into the fabric. Connect the corners, and sew along this triangle. Next, cut from the center to the seam.
32. Open the strip and place one edge towards the left and the other towards the right. Then fold the strip lengthwise and you will see a V forming from the seam.
33. Align the corner of the raw edge with the corner of the neckline strip. Make a few stitches to secure in place. Then align the raw edges together and start sewing along with a zigzag stitch.

34. As you are about to finish sewing all around the neckline, keep the raw edges aligned. Once you reach the beginning, finish the stitch and turn the strip inward.
35. Working with a twin needle is fun once you let go of your fear of this scary looking needle. After getting familiarized with the possibilities of the twin needle, you won't be able to imagine a sewing life without it.
36. A twin needle is made of two needles combined into one. On the surface, it creates two perfectly parallel stitches while on the wrong side it forms a zigzag stitch to secure the raw edge. Twin needles are perfect for knit projects that should look more professional.
37. To thread a twin needle, you will need two spools for the top threading. Your sewing machine will have two shafts on which you can place the spools.
38. Thread the machine as you normally would, but in this instance, you'll pull both threads at the same time. Once you reach the needle, you will insert one thread into each eye.
39. When working with twin needles, you are going to stitch on the right side of the fabric. This way your parallel stitches will be visible. On the incorrect side of the canvas, you will find the zigzag dot. Hem the sleeves and the bottom edge with the twin needles.

Apron with Pockets
Materials

- 1 x 1 yards of woven fabric (i.e. cotton, denim, flax)
- Measurement tape
- Tailor's chalk
- Ruler

What's new:

- Sewing front pockets
- Attaching long bias strips

Directions

1. There are a few pieces you need to cut out - the body, a rectangular pocket and a long bias strip. To cut the pieces, you first want to trace them on a sheet of paper, or you can just measure and trace straight onto the fabric.
2. Fold your fabric in half so as to accommodate a width of 13 ½" and a length of 30".
3. From the top of the fabric, measure 6" horizontally and mark that spot. Then measure 8" vertically along the folded edge of the fabric and make a marking. From there, measure 13 ½" horizontally towards the center of the fabric and mark. Unite the two marks from the two horizontal lines with a curved line.
4. From the 8" line, go down another 22" on both sides of the fabric and unite the lines. This will result in a total length of 30". Cut out the piece.
5. For the pocket, all you need is a 14" x 23" square.
6. For the bias tape, you need one strip of 70" by 2". If your fabric cannot accommodate this length (see

SEWING: GRANDMA'S SPECIAL TRICKS

picture), simply cut two 35" x 2" strips. Later you will be able to join them together to form a long strip.

7. Starting with the bias strip, fold the sides towards the middle line, then press and repeat the process on the other edge.
8. Fold the two sides together so they overlap, then press once again.
9. Moving on to the pocket piece, press 3 sides inwards to about ¾". The upper part will be pressed into a double fold, 1 ¼" each time.
10. Stitch the double-folded hem of the pocket with a straight stitch.
11. Reaching the corner, include the pressed raw edge into the seam.
12. Position your pocket to your preferred height, then pin it onto the apron, the incorrect side of the pouch facing the right side of the apron. The raw, pressed edges of the pocket will have to be inside the pocket itself.
13. Top stitch the pocket on the three sides with 1/8" seam.
14. Then you have the option to split the large pocket into two medium-sized pockets by simply sewing the top along the center line.
15. Double fold inwards, ½", all the raw edges except the curved armhole edges, pin them into place and sew with a straight stitch.
16. Reaching the corners, simply lift the presser foot and gently turn the fabric to a 90° angle, place the presser foot back down and continue sewing.
17. If, as mentioned previously, you have two pieces of

bias, you will want to combine them into one long strip.
18. Open up the ends of the strips and place them together right sides facing. Make a straight stitch.
19. Then open up the strip and make a rectangular top stitch. This will secure the raw edges into place and flatten out the strip.
20. Close back the bias tape and prepare to attach it to the apron.
21. From the center of the bias strip, measure 10" and pin that spot to the top corner of the apron.
22. Pin the bias tape along the curved raw edge. Make sure you open up the bias tape in order to sandwich the raw edge of the apron between the two pleats of the bias tape.
23. Repeat the process on the other side of the apron. Measure again 10" and pin the bias onto the outer corner. Continue pinning all along the curved edge, with the raw curved edge sandwiched between the pleats.
24. Top stitch all along the bias strip, from one end to the other. Use a straight stitch about 1/8" from the inner edge.
25. Close the ends of the bias strip by folding them inwards, then stitching on top.

Washcloth Ducky
Materials

- Washcloth
- Thread
- Washcloth duck template

- Felt paper in black and orange

Directions

1. Enlarge and print template.
2. Cut duck shapes out of the template on a washcloth and make sure to use solid lines so you can create 2 ducks. A single oval will make the base then you will cut two identical shapes on the sponge for the head and two more shapes for the tail. Make body thicker by cutting more sponge, then cut two more shapes for the wings.
3. Take two of the body pieces then sew them together but make sure to leave the bottom open and stuff it with sponges after turning right side out. Hand sew after covering the hole with an oval shaped piece, and then sew the wings but leave the bottoms open again. Stuff with sponges then sew on wings by hand.
4. Sew black knots out of thread onto the face to create the eyes of the duck then cut two oval shaped pieces from felt paper to create the bill. Use orange thread to stitch it on.
5. Now, your washcloth ducky is ready!
6. Enjoy!

Gingham Coasters
Materials

- Gingham scraps, cut into 3 ½ inch squares
- Iron-on vinyl
- Solid cotton scraps, cut into 3 ½ inch squares

- Sewing supplies
- Sewing machine

Directions

1. Sew gingham scraps onto the cotton scraps and leave ½ inch seam allowance.
2. Press vinyl onto the gingham, following the instructions on the package.
3. Trim edges by leaving ¼ inch space on seams.
4. Enjoy!

iPod Case

Materials

Needle and thread/sewing machine

- Erasable fabric marker
- Mini scissors
- 9 x 3 to 5/8 inch fabric
- iPod cover pattern

Directions

1. Download and print iPod cover pattern then cut the rectangular and circular holes.
2. Pin pattern to the fabric and use pen to trace the openings then cut them out.
3. Fold the fabric in half from one end to the other then sew after pinning to hold in place. Make sure to leave ¼ inch allowance.
4. Enjoy!

SEWING: GRANDMA'S SPECIAL TRICKS

Reusable Tunic for Kids

Materials

- Fabric with designs of your own choice
- Thread
- Needles
- Scissors
- Tunic pattern
- Double adhesive tape

Directions

1. First, make sure that you have washed and dried the fabric before using it.
2. Download and print pattern at 100% then use double adhesive tape to stick it to the fabric.
3. You can also trace the pattern onto the fabric by using baking paper and fabric chalk to mark linings.
4. Cut the pieces so you have the front of the dress, the back of the dress, neck facing, sleeves, pockets pieces, and pocket linings.
5. Then, make neck pleats by transferring pleat markings onto the fabric and pinning together before stitching. Use slip stitches to sew the pleats, and then press down.
6. To make the pockets, mark them with 5 x 1 cm lines. Pin the outer marked lines on the center and press pleats on the bottom of the angles of the top folds all the way to the bottom folds. Pin linings to the center until you see the rectangular part of the pocket. Sew around it to leave at least 3 cm

opening before clipping and creating rounded edges. Note that a finished pocket will resemble the top edge has been pressed underneath so you can easily attach it to the dress. Pin pockets to dress before sewing.
7. Next, let shoulder seams come together by sewing right and front parts together before pressing down.
8. Now, make the neckline by pinning the neck overlock to the right sides of the neckline then sew around the curve of the neck. Open one side up and leave 3 cm of space before looping and sewing other pieces together.
9. To make the sleeves, turn and over-lock the sleeves together then sew under the edge before pressing.
10. Attach sleeves to the dress by sewing next to the curve and then bind the two rows together.
11. To sew the back seam, place pins on the back then sew all the way to the button before pressing down. Then over-lock with the button and leave at least 2 cm of space before using iron for pressing.
12. Sew everything together and enjoy!

Ruffled Ombre Dress
Materials

- A large piece of cotton cloth
- Extra fabric, for ruffles
- Thread
- Needle
- Scissors
- Dress pattern

SEWING: GRANDMA'S SPECIAL TRICKS

Directions

1. Download and enlarge pattern. Around 100 to 300% will work.
2. Trace the dress pattern onto the fabric then cut it out.
3. Fold then cut, but make sure you don't go overboard by cutting the shoulders then make ruffles by cutting strips of fabric. It would be nice if you could have various colors around then sew them to the hem of the bodice. Pin them first to keep them in place then make sure to cut at the back, when necessary. Use running or zigzag stitches for this one.
4. Then, place the front and back sides of the fabric together and sew the edges to make them one piece of cloth.
5. Fold the edge and make some slip stitches to make way for the arm hole.
6. Then, take some more fabric and cut two strips. Stitch them together to create a long stripe.
7. Sew the rest of the ends together and make sure to hem the bottom, as well, to create the notion that the piece has a circular feel to it.
8. Use basting stitches for the strip of ruffles then case around the strip with the use of an elastic strip to leave ¼ inch space. Make sure that the elastic is durable enough for the dress.
9. The space will then serve as the opening where you can insert the elastic. Widen it to your desired length before stitching the two ends together and before stitching the opening of the casing.

10. That's it—you now have your ruffled ombre dress!

Halter Top Dress
Materials

- Halter top pattern
- Large piece of cloth
- Scissors
- Thread
- Needle
- Iron
- Bias tape

Directions

1. Enlarge the pattern by 100% then download, print, and trace on the fabric. Add length, if needed.
2. Cut one shell and one lining of the fabric after pinning it down.
3. Then cut some straps that are around 1.5 x 9 inch in size.
4. Cut a rectangular piece of fabric to serve as the skirt then add 2 inches to the waist before cutting and measuring down to your desired length. Then, cut one more shell for the underskirt and add 2 inches, as well.
5. Pin the straps on the shell, just on the right side, and stitch right sides together all the way to the neck to reinforce the straps before pressing then turn the fabric right side out and press again.
6. Align the sides to the back then stitch using elastic

SEWING: GRANDMA'S SPECIAL TRICKS

thread between the fabric lining and the seam of the shell.

7. Sew some baste stitches, either by hand or with a machine, to attach the bottom.
8. Attach midpoint of straps to the neckline, using bias tape. Fold bias to finish the strap.
9. Now, sew the sides of the skirt to the shell and the underskirt. Make sure that you baste the lining and make sure that the right sides are on an upward position.
10. Sew remaining edges and cut excess.
11. That's it—you now have a lovely halter top dress!

CONCLUSIONS

Sewing has become a worldwide art, where millions of customers and individual consumers are served each day, with different kinds of products, using sewing techniques. Sewing is no more a manual and traditional task. It has become a complete digital and computerized technique. This is because of different kinds of machines and tools that are based on different kinds of sophisticated technology. With this advancement, sewing has become a passion for several people around the globe. We have written this book, keeping in mind the interest of several our readers.

All the types of techniques are elaborately discussed so that the readers can easily choose the appropriate technique, according to the type of fabric and the pattern to be made. We hope that we have become successful in elaborating all the important issues to our readers, so that the manuscript can serve as the complete guide to the sewing practice.

Now, new and enhanced designs and patterns have been used in order to give advanced looks to outfits. Extra time can be utilized in creating something beautiful so it is a good

CONCLUSIONS

activity for spending leisure time. Sewing can be used for earning revenue also. Family income could be supplemented by sewing. It also can be adopted as small or medium-term businesses. There is a tremendous style for different dresses. Simple to complex projects can be handled with this art. In fact, sewing is the basis for every stylish item.

www.ingramcontent.com/pod-product-compliance
Lightning Source LLC
Chambersburg PA
CBHW070942080526
44589CB00013B/1609